FRENCH
FOR BEGINNERS
WORKBOOK
Meeting People and Traveling

Rachel Bladon

Illustrated by John Shackell

Designed by Diane Thistlethwaite

Language consultant: Anita Herbert

Series editor: Nicole Irving

CONTENTS

le chat

la maison

la clef

la fille

le soleil

la voiture

le chien

Greetings and making friends

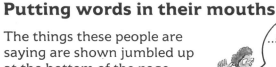

Here and on the next two pages you can practice greeting people and asking their names. All the French words you will need are shown in the Word checks and the pictures.

Word check

salut	hi, hello, bye
bonjour	hello, good morning/afternoon
bonsoir	good evening
au revoir	goodbye

Salut means "hi" or "bye." You only use it for someone you know well or someone your own age.

When talking to an adult you don't know well, it is polite to add **Monsieur** (Mr.) or **Madame** (Mrs.) to your greeting, for example **Bonjour, Madame**. You say **Monsieur** to a man and **Madame** to a woman.

ça va?	how are you?, are you all right?
ça va bien	fine
pas très bien	not very well
je m'appelle	My name is
il/elle s'appelle	his/her name is
elles	they (when talking about girls or women)
ils	they (for boys or men, or boys and girls together)
ils/elles s'appellent	their names are
comment tu t'appelles?	what is your name?
comment il/elle s'appelle?	what is his/her name?
comment ils/elles s'appellent?	what are their names?
et	and

Putting words in their mouths

The things these people are saying are shown jumbled up at the bottom of the page. Can you unscramble the words and fill in each empty speech bubble with the right French greeting?*

A. au Revoir

Ça va?

B. Pas tres bien

C. Bonjour Monsieur

Ça va?

D. ça va bien

E. Salut

F. Bonjour Madame

G. au revoir

NAVEBIAÇ
TULSA
ÈSERPITNABS
RUMBISSNONOOIER
MOEDJANBOMRUA
VURRAOIE
ROVUIREA

*The answers to this puzzle and all the puzzles in this book are on pages 28 to 30.

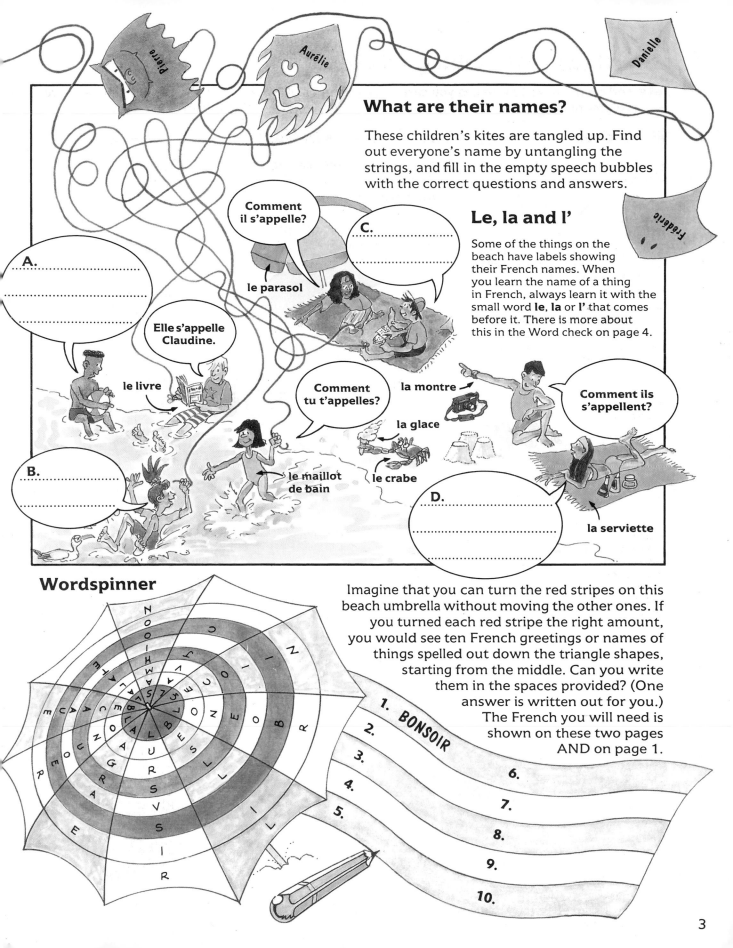

What are their names?

These children's kites are tangled up. Find out everyone's name by untangling the strings, and fill in the empty speech bubbles with the correct questions and answers.

Le, la and l'

Some of the things on the beach have labels showing their French names. When you learn the name of a thing in French, always learn it with the small word **le**, **la** or **l'** that comes before it. There is more about this in the Word check on page 4.

Wordspinner

Imagine that you can turn the red stripes on this beach umbrella without moving the other ones. If you turned each red stripe the right amount, you would see ten French greetings or names of things spelled out down the triangle shapes, starting from the middle. Can you write them in the spaces provided? (One answer is written out for you.) The French you will need is shown on these two pages AND on page 1.

1. BONSOIR
2.
3.
4.
5.
6.
7.
8.
9.
10.

More greetings and introductions

Here are some more puzzles to practice greetings and nouns (words for things).

Word check

French has two words for "you," **tu** and **vous**. **Tu** is what you say to a friend, a relative or someone your own age. You use **vous** for an adult you don't know well, and for more than one person.

comment tu t'appelles?,	what is your name?
comment vous vous appelez?	

All French words for things (nouns) are either "masculine" or "feminine." The word for "the" is **le** before masculine nouns and **la** before feminine ones, but before nouns that begin with "a," "e," "i," "o" or "u," it is always **l'**.

In word lists, [m] or [f] after a **l'** noun tells you if it is masculine or feminine. You always learn nouns with the right word for "the."

le stylo	pen
la carte	map
l'appareil-photo [m]	camera
l'église [f]	church

"A" or "an" is **un** before masculine nouns (**un stylo** – a pen) and **une** before feminine ones (**une église** – a church).

Lost for words

Rob is visiting Paris. He is trying to practice his French. What should he say in these situations? Circle the correct answer A, B or C.

1. He wants to buy something for breakfast. How should he greet the store clerk?

A. **Salut.**
B. **Bonjour, Madame.**
C. **Bonjour, Monsieur.** (circled)

2. In the shop, Rob meets a girl who is staying at the same youth hostel as him. How should he say "hello"?

A. **Bonjour, Madame.**
B. **Bonsoir.**
C. **Salut.** (circled)

3. He asks the girl her name.

A. **Comment tu t'appelles?** (circled)
B. **Comment elle s'appelle?**
C. **Comment vous vous appelez?**

4. Rob has to meet his pen pal at the top of the Eiffel Tower, so he says "goodbye" to the girl.

A. **Bonjour, Madame.**
B. **Salut.**
C. **Bonsoir.**

5. He is late and the elevators up the Eiffel Tower are out of order. When he finally reaches the top, his friend asks, "**Ça va?**" How does he answer?

A. **Pas très bien.**
B. **Salut.**
C. **Ça va bien.**

Word search

Hidden in each grid are the French names of seven things. Can you find them and complete the labels for each grid (adding the right word for "the")? The first label is filled in for you.*

*For this and all the puzzles in this workbook, you may need French words that are shown on earlier pages.

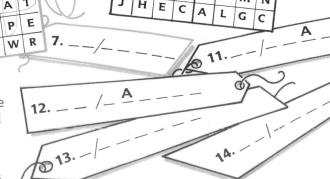

1. L E / C R A B E
2. La / V O I T U R E car?
3. ? La / C h a t
4. _ _ / _ _ _ _ _ _ _
5. Le / c h i e n
6. La / P A R A S O L
7. _ _ _ / _ _ _ _ _
8. _ _ _ / _ O _ _ _ _ _
9. _ _ _ / _ T _ _ _
10. _ _ _ / _ I _ _
11. _ _ / _ A _ _ _
12. _ _ / _ A _ _ _ _
13. _ / _ _ _ _
14. _ _ / _ _ _ _

Word search grid 1:
A C H I E N L V
F P A E B U O S
N C B R I I S M
A R L P T C A B
M A A U S E R I
C B R O C H A T
T E D H L L P E
E R T N O M W R

Word search grid 2:
E L A R B G I D
A E S O I F N M
P S O L E I L A
E I T B R L D I
W L F Y H L F S
C G L T L E F O
F É U A L O M N
J H E C A L G C

Lost and found

Pierre is going into the forest to look for six things that he dropped there. (You can see them all on the map.) At each signpost there is a strange creature. To find his belongings, Pierre must always follow the sign that shows the right answer to what the creature is saying. Can you list (in French, using the right words for "the") his six things in the order he picks them up?

The six things that Pierre picks up:

1. ....
2. ....
3. ....
4. ....
5. ....
6. ....

Numbers and saying your age

These puzzles are about saying how old you are and counting up to twenty.

Word check

Here is the French action word, **avoir** (to have). Like all verbs, it changes (has slightly different words) when different people do the action.

avoir	to have
j'ai	I have
tu as	you have
il/elle a	he/she has
nous avons	we have
vous avez	you have
ils/elles ont	they have

The French for "I," **je**, turns into **j'** before words that begin with "a," "e," "i," "o" and "u."

To say how old you are in French, you say how many years you "have," so you use **avoir**.

quel âge as-tu?	how old are you?
j'ai . . . ans	I am . . . years old
j'ai dix ans	I am ten years old

Numbers

1	**un, une**	11	**onze**
2	**deux**	12	**douze**
3	**trois**	13	**treize**
4	**quatre**	14	**quatorze**
5	**cinq**	15	**quinze**
6	**six**	16	**seize**
7	**sept**	17	**dix-sept**
8	**huit**	18	**dix-huit**
9	**neuf**	19	**dix-neuf**
10	**dix**	20	**vingt**

"One" is **un** before masculine words and **une** before feminine words.

When you are talking about more than one thing, you add "s" to the end of most French nouns, and the word for "the" is always **les**.

l'île [f]	island
les îles	islands

How old are they?

These children are talking about how old they are. (Their ages are shown on their clothes.) Find what they are saying in the panel on the side of the tent and fill in the speech bubbles. (You will not need everything in the panel.)

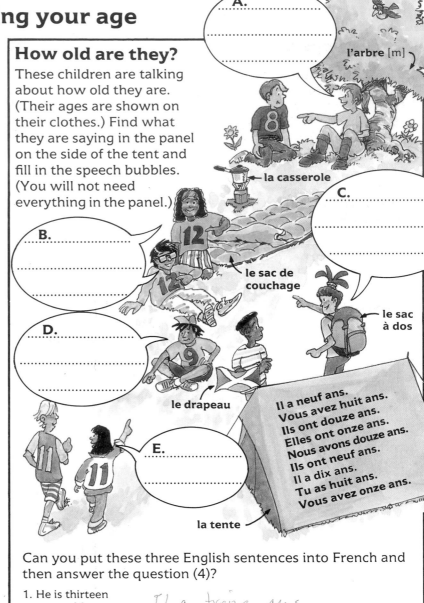

A.

l'arbre [m]

la casserole

C.

B.

le sac de couchage

le sac à dos

D.

le drapeau

E.

Il a neuf ans.
Vous avez huit ans.
Ils ont douze ans.
Elles ont onze ans.
Nous avons douze ans.
Ils ont neuf ans.
Il a dix ans.
Tu as huit ans.
Vous avez onze ans.

la tente

Can you put these three English sentences into French and then answer the question (4)?

1. He is thirteen years old. _Il a treize ans_
2. She is ten years old. _Elle a dix ans_
3. We are eleven years old. _Nous avons onze ans_
4. **Quel âge as-tu?** _J'ai 10 ans_

l'Île Verte

Island hoppers

Frédéric and Claudine have each visited three of these islands. They made lists of what they spotted but they both left out one thing. Can you add the missing thing to each list and write the names of the islands they visited in their notebooks?

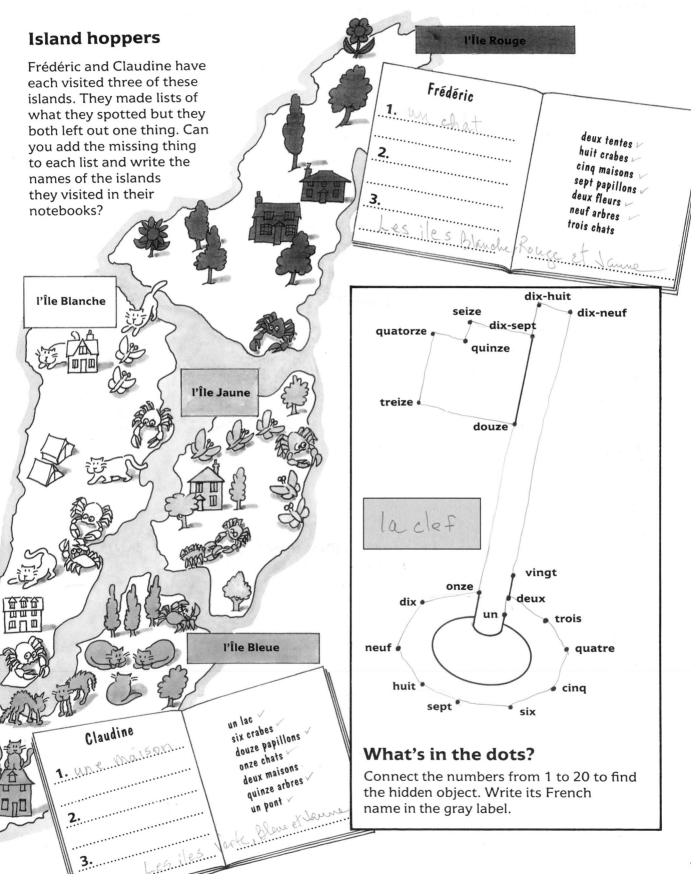

l'Île Rouge

Frédéric

1. un chat

2.

3.

Les îles Blanche, Rouge et Jaune

deux tentes ✓
huit crabes ✓
cinq maisons ✓
sept papillons ✓
deux fleurs ✓
neuf arbres ✓
trois chats

l'Île Blanche

l'Île Jaune

l'Île Bleue

Claudine

1. une maison

2.

3.

Les îles Verte, Bleue et Jaune

un lac ✓
six crabes ✓
douze papillons ✓
onze chats
deux maisons ✓
quinze arbres ✓
un pont

dix-huit
seize
dix-sept
quatorze
quinze
treize
douze
dix-neuf

la clef

vingt
onze
deux
dix
un
trois
neuf
quatre
huit
cinq
sept
six

What's in the dots?

Connect the numbers from 1 to 20 to find the hidden object. Write its French name in the gray label.

7

Where do you come from?

Here you will find puzzles for you to practice talking about where you are from.

Countries

l'Allemagne [f]	Germany
l'Angleterre [f]	England
l'Australie [f]	Australia
l'Autriche [f]	Austria
la Chine	China
la Corse	Corsica
l'Écosse [f]	Scotland
l'Espagne [f]	Spain
les États-Unis	the United States
la France	France
la Norvège	Norway
les Pays-Bas	the Netherlands
le pays de Galles	Wales

Word check

Here is the action word **venir** (to come):

je viens	I come
tu viens	you come
il/elle vient	he/she/it comes
nous venons	we come
vous venez	you come
ils/elles viennent	they come

For "it" in French, you use **il** to talk about a masculine word and **elle** to talk about a feminine one. For "they," you use **elles** for a feminine word. You use **ils** for a masculine word, and for masculine and feminine words together.

d'où?	where ... from?
tu viens d'où?,	where do you
vous venez d'où?	come from?
ils/elles viennent	where do they
d'où?	come from?

To say where you come from, you use **de** (from) in front of **la** countries. **De** turns into **du** with **le** countries, **d'** with **l'** countries and **des** with **les** countries. In each case, you drop **le**, **la**, **l'** and **les**.

je viens de France	I come from France
tu viens du pays de Galles	you come from Wales
ils/elles viennent d'Angleterre	they come from England
elle vient des Pays-Bas	she comes from the Netherlands

Around the world

Can you fill in the empty labels on these countries with their French names?

Now look at the map and fill in the spaces on the right saying which country the characters come from. Begin each answer with the French for "he," "she," "it" or "they."

B. l'Écosse

C. la Norvège

le mouton

le cheval

la baleine

A. le pays de Galles

la souris

D. l'Angleterre

le hérisson

le Danemark

E. les Pays-Bas

l'Irlande [f]

le cochon

H. l'Allemagne

la Belgique

le serpent

F. l'Espagne

G. la France

I. l'Autriche

le Luxembourg

la Suisse

la vache

le Portugal

J. la Corse

la Sardaigne

le lapin

l'Italie [f]

la Sicile

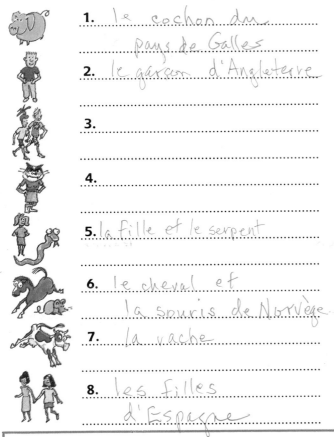

1. le cochon du pays de Galles
2. le garçon d'Angleterre
3.
4.
5. la fille et le serpent
6. le cheval et la souris de Norvège
7. la vache
8. les filles d'Espagne

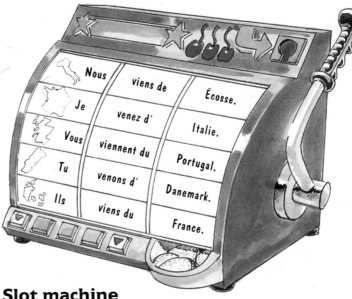

Slot machine

Someone has played on the slot machine and jumbled up the last two parts of each sentence. Can you sort them out and complete the yellow box below?

Nous	venons d'Italie
Je	viens de France
Vous	venez d'Écosse
Tu	viens du Portugal
Ils	viennent du Danemark

Use the clues to fill in the crossword. (Don't forget the different words for "a" or "the.")*

Across:
1. It shines on summer days. (2, 6)
7. You might use it to get across a river. (2, 4)
8. You can get milk from one. (3, 5)
10. "The" before feminine nouns. (2)
11. "They" (girls or women). (5)
12. "A" before feminine nouns. (3)
15. Its capital city is Peking. (2, 5)
16. "They" (boys or men). (3)
17. You might see a bullfight in this country. (1, 7)
18. "You" (for someone you know well). (2)

Down:
1. You only use this umbrella when it is sunny. (2, 7)
2. "Hello" (for someone you know well). (5)
3. You might sleep inside it if you went camping. (2, 5)
4. The French for "he." (2)
5. You use them to unlock doors. (3, 5)
6. The French for "and." (2)
9. This country is famous for watches and chocolate. (2, 6)
10. "The" before masculine nouns. (2)
12. A witch might have a black one. (2, 4)
13. Pierre's age (see pages 3 and 6). (4)
14. 2 × 10. (5)

*Remember that to do the puzzles in this book, you may need French words that are shown on earlier pages.

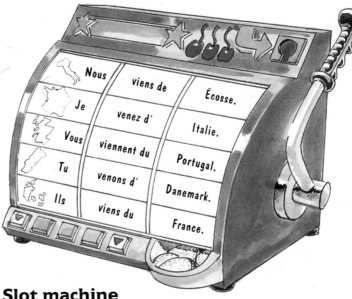 9

Talking about your family

On these two pages you can practice talking about your family.

Family names

la famille	family
le frère	brother
la soeur	sister
le père	father
la mère	mother
les parents [m]	parents
la grand-mère	grandmother
le grand-père	grandfather
les grands-parents [m]	grandparents
le mari	husband
la femme	wife
l'oncle [m]	uncle
la tante	aunt
le cousin	cousin (boy or man)
la cousine	cousin (girl or woman)

Word check

Here is the action word **être** (to be):

je suis	I am
tu es	you are
il/elle est	he/she/it is
nous sommes	we are
vous êtes	you are
ils/elles sont	they are

The French words for "my" and "his" or "her" are different depending on whether they are used with **le**, **la**, **l'** or **les** nouns. Here you can see which word to use:

	my	his/her
with **le** or **l'** nouns	**mon**	**son**
with **la** nouns	**ma**	**sa**
with **les** nouns	**mes**	**ses**

mon chat	my cat
sa carte	his/her map
mes clefs	my keys

In French, for expressions like "Marc's aunt," you use **de** (from, of) and say "the aunt of Marc":

Marie est la tante de Marc	Marie is Marc's aunt

Family connections

Use the clues below to fill in the name labels on the Champagne family tree. Then answer the questions in French, making full sentences with the words for "is" or "are." Put your answers at the bottom of the page.

Jacques est le père de Dominique.
Bernadette est la femme de Jacques.
Guy est le frère de Jacques.
Jacques est l'oncle de Claudine.
Monique est la soeur de Claudine et Frédéric.
Françoise est la grand-mère de Dominique.
Jean est le mari de Françoise.
Francine est la tante de Dominique et Marc.

1. Who are Guy's parents?
2. Who is Claudine's grandfather?
3. Who is Dominique's mother?
4. Who is Marc's uncle?

La Famille Champagne

A. Jean
B. Françoise
C. Bernadette
D. Francine
E. Jacques
F. Guy
G. Marc
H. Frédéric
I. Dominique
J. Monique
Claudine

1. ....
2. ....
3. ....
4. ....

Word cross

Use the clues below to write the correct French words across the grid, with the right word for "a." Your answers will spell the name of a relative down the gray column. Write the English for it in the space below.

1. It likes cheese.
2. This one has 32 pages.
3. A tulip is one.
4. It has four wheels.
5. It produces milk.
6. You need one to tell the time.
7. It goes from a gate to a front door.
8. It is surrounded by water.

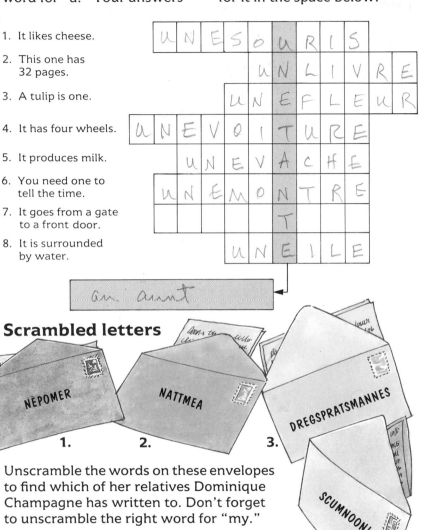

Grid answers:
1. UNE SOURIS
2. UN LIVRE
3. UNE FLEUR
4. UNE VOITURE
5. UNE VACHE
6. UNE MONTRE
8. UNE ILE

an. aunt

Scrambled letters

1. NEPOMER
2. NATTMEA
3. DREGSPRATSMANNES
4. SCUMNOONI

Unscramble the words on these envelopes to find which of her relatives Dominique Champagne has written to. Don't forget to unscramble the right word for "my."

Who on the Champagne family tree will not get letters from Dominique? List them in French (using the right word for "her").

The writing on the envelopes says:	Dominique did not write to:
1. Mon pere	1. ma grandmère
2. ma tante	2. mon oncle
3. mes grandsparents	3. mes parents
4. mon cousin	4. ma cousine

Spot the mistakes

Marc Champagne has tried to write about his family, but he has made two mistakes in each sentence. Can you spot his mistakes and write the sentences out correctly in the spaces below?

1. Bernadette es mon mère.
2. Guy sont ma oncle.
3. Monique est Claudine sont mes cousins.
4. Jean et Françoise suis ma grands-parents.
5. Je sommes le soeur de Dominique.
6. Monique et Claudine sommes la soeurs de Frédéric.
7. Frédéric est ma cousine.

1. ma
2. est
3. et
4. sont
5. suis
6. sont
7. mon cousin

11

Getting to know people

These puzzles will help you describe people in French and get to know them.

Word check

le pantalon	pants
la jupe	skirt
la robe	dress
le pull	sweater
la chemise	shirt
cher	dear (to start a letter to a boy or man)
chère	dear (for a girl or woman)
grosses bises	love (to end a letter)

To describe people or things in French, you often use slightly different words depending on whether you are talking about masculine or feminine nouns.

Below is a list of masculine describing words. The letters after them show what you add to make them feminine:

petit(e)	short, small
grand(e)	tall, large
brun(e)	dark
blond(e)	blond
vert(e)	green
bleu(e)	blue
noir(e)	black
blanc(he)	white

Some describing words are the same for masculine and feminine nouns, for example:

rouge	red
jaune	yellow

Odd ones out

Read Aurélie's descriptions of her friends on the blue sheet below. Can you put their names in the right labels on the picture? (Two will stay empty.)

A. Flavien

l'assiette [f]

la table

la salade

la saucisse

la chaise

B. Margot

C. Marc

D. Isabelle

le verre

la fourchette

E. Nathalie

F. Céline

le jus d'orange

G. Guillaume

H. Sylvain

I. Claire

J. Yves

Aurélie has left out Claire and Marc. Fill in their labels and write a sentence about each one's height and hair on the blue sheet. (Begin your answers with **Il** or **Elle**.)

Flavien est brun. Sa chemise est noire. Céline est grande et blonde. Nathalie est grande et brune. Sa jupe est bleue. Sylvain est grand et blond. Son pull est vert. Isabelle est grande et brune. Sa robe est jaune. Yves est petit et blond. Son pull est rouge. Margot est petite et brune. Guillaume est petit et blond. Son pantalon est blanc.

Il est gran et brun. Son pull est bleu.
Elle est blonde. Son pantalon est bleu.

Aurélie

Clipped sentences

The answers to the questions below have been cut into two or three pieces and mixed up. Can you fit the pieces back together and write the answers in the correct place in the green box?

1. **Il vient d'où?**
2. **Quel âge as-tu?**
3. **Comment elle s'appelle?**
4. **Ça va?**
5. **Comment elles s'appellent?**
6. **Vous venez d'où?**
7. **Comment ils s'appellent?**
8. **Tu viens d'où?**

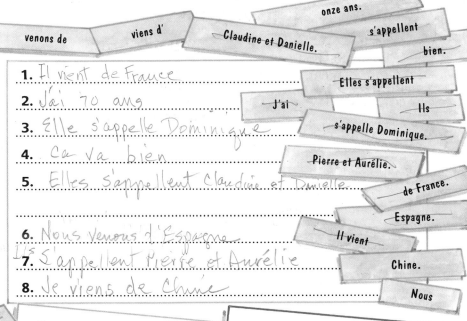

1. Il vient de France
2. J'ai 70 ans
3. Elle s'appelle Dominique
4. Ça va bien
5. Elles s'appellent Claudine et Danielle

6. Nous venons d'Espagne
7. Ils s'appellent Pierre et Aurélie
8. Je viens de Chine

Postcard to a pen pal

On the right are postcards that Vicky and her new French pen pal have written to each other. Put Danielle's card into English and Vicky's into French. (Write in the spaces below.)

Chère Vicky,

Ça va? Je m'appelle Danielle et j'ai douze ans. Je viens de France. J'ai une soeur et un chat. Ma soeur s'appelle Aline. Elle a neuf ans. Je suis grande et brune, et ma soeur est petite et brune. Quel âge as-tu?

Grosses bises,
Danielle

Dear Danielle,

My name is Vicky. I'm eleven years old and I come from the United States. I am tall and blond. I have one brother. His name is Nick and he is thirteen years old. I have two sisters. Their names are Alison and Lucy. They are seven years old.

Love,
Vicky

Dear Vicky,
How are you? My name is Danielle and I am 12yrs old. I am from France. I have a sister and a cat. My sister's name is Aline. She is 9yrs old. I am tall and brunette, and my sister is small and brunette. How old are you?
Love,
Danielle

Chère Danielle,
Je m'appelle Vicky. J'ai onze ans et je viens d'États-Unis. Je suis grande et blonde. J'ai un frère. Il s'appelle Nick, et il a treize ans. J'ai deux soeurs. Elles s'appellent Alison et Lucy. Elles ont sept ans.
Grosses bises,
Vicky

What time is it?

These puzzles are all about action words and telling the time.

Word check

Here is the action word **arriver** (to arrive):

j'arrive	I arrive
tu arrives	you arrive
il/elle arrive	he/she/it arrives
nous arrivons	we arrive
vous arrivez	you arrive
ils/elles arrivent	they arrive

Most action words that end in "er" (like the three below) change in the same way as **arriver** when different people do the action:

quitter	to leave
rentrer	to go back, to go home
jouer (au football)	to play (soccer)
après	after
avec	with
à	to, at
l'école [f]	school
l'ami [m]	friend (boy, man)
l'amie [f]	friend (girl, woman)
le déjeuner	lunch

Telling the time

quelle heure est-il?	what time is it?
il est une heure	it is one o'clock
il est huit heures	it is eight o'clock

There is no word for "after" or "past" in French. You just say the hour and add the number of minutes:

il est huit heures cinq it is five after eight

For "to," you say the hour and add **moins** (minus) and the number of minutes:

il est neuf heures moins dix it is ten to nine

quatre heures et quart	a quarter after four
trois heures et demie	three thirty
dix heures moins le quart	a quarter to ten
à (six heures)	at (six o'clock)
midi	noon, twelve o'clock

Clockwork

Four of these clocks are not showing the time. Draw hands on their clockfaces to show the times given on the labels. Then fill in the empty labels for the clocks that are showing the time.

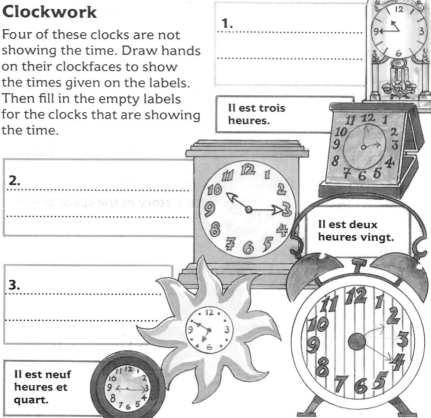

1. ....

Il est trois heures.

2. ....

Il est deux heures vingt.

3. ....

Il est neuf heures et quart.

Word circle

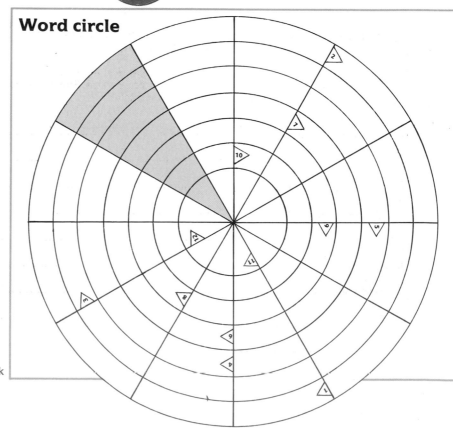

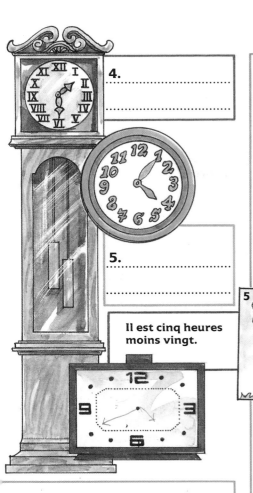

4. ....

....

5. ....

....

Il est cinq heures moins vingt.

A day in the life

Jean and Philippe both come from Paris, are the same age and look very similar. Read about Jean and decide which picture from each pair is of him. Put the numbers of these pictures in the order of the story and write them in the red box.

The other five pictures are of Philippe. Use them to rewrite the story in the space below so that it is now about him.

Jean vient de Paris. Il a douze ans, il est grand et brun. Il a un frère et deux soeurs.

Il quitte la maison à sept heures et demie.

Il arrive à l'école à huit heures moins cinq.

Après le déjeuner, il joue au football avec son ami. Son ami est petit et blond.

Il quitte l'école à quatre heures vingt.

....
....
....
....
....
....
....
....
....
....

Write the things below in French around the circle, putting the first letter of each one next to its number. Your answers will spell out a new bit of French in the gray section. Put the English for it in the gray label.

1. I GO HOME
2. YOU HAVE (to a friend)
3. WE ARRIVE
4. YOU COME (to an adult you don't know well)
5. I HAVE
6. I ARRIVE
7. HE IS
8. SHE PLAYS
9. YOU ARE (to a friend)
10. WE LEAVE
11. HE HAS
12. THEY PLAY (boys or men)

Getting around

On these two pages you can practice useful things to say when you travel around France.

Word check

l'aller simple [m] one way (ticket)
l'aller-retour [m] round trip (ticket)
le trajet trip
le trajet jusqu'à ... the trip to ...
  dure (deux heures) takes (two hours)
la minute minute
l'heure [f] hour

Aller (to go) is an action word that ends in "er," but does not change in the same way as **arriver** (on page 14):

je vais I go
tu vas you go
il/elle va he/she/it goes
nous allons we go
vous allez you go
ils/elles vont they go

acheter to buy
s'il vous plaît please
oui yes
non no
ou or
merci thank you
mais but
pour for, to
le prix price
c'est combien? how much is it/that?
ça coûte it/that costs

French money: there are 100 **centimes** in **un franc**.

Numbers 21-100

21	vingt et un	32	trente-deux	72	soixante-douze
22	vingt-deux	33	trente-trois	80	quatre-vingts
23	vingt-trois	40	quarante	81	quatre-vingt-un
24	vingt-quatre	50	cinquante	82	quatre-vingt-deux
25	vingt-cinq	60	soixante	90	quatre-vingt-dix
30	trente	70	soixante-dix	91	quatre-vingt-onze
31	trente et un	71	soixante et onze	100	cent

Time travelers

Can you complete this story about Debbie and Bill's trip to France? Put a number next to each piece of French in the box (below left) to show which blank it fits into.

When Debbie and Bill arrived in Calais, they went to the station to buy tickets to Boulerque. On the way, an old lady asked them "......1......" Debbie looked at her watch and replied "......2......" The lady seemed surprised.

"......3......," Debbie said politely to the man at the ticket office. "......4......," she said, adding: "......5......" "......6......," the man replied, handing her a round-trip ticket. "......7......," he said as he took Debbie's 66 francs.

Bill had arranged to stay in Boulerque. "......8......," he said. "......9......," the man said, taking Bill's 50 franc note and handing him back 17 francs. Debbie asked what time the train for Boulerque would leave Calais. "......10......," he replied.

As they had nearly an hour and a half to spare, Debbie and Bill went to a café. Hearing them speak in English, the waiter inquired, "......11......" "......12......," they replied. They chatted with him for a long time, then Debbie looked at her watch and got up hastily. "......13......," she explained to the waiter. He frowned and said that the last train to Boulerque had already left. "......14......," Bill said. The waiter laughed, shaking his head, and pointed at the clock: "......15......" Debbie and Bill groaned. Of course! They had forgotten to change their watches to French time!

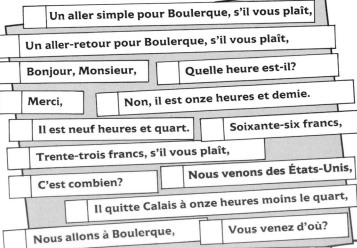

Un aller simple pour Boulerque, s'il vous plaît,

Un aller-retour pour Boulerque, s'il vous plaît,

Bonjour, Monsieur,

Quelle heure est-il?

Merci,

Non, il est onze heures et demie.

Il est neuf heures et quart.

Soixante-six francs,

Trente-trois francs, s'il vous plaît,

C'est combien?

Nous venons des États-Unis,

Il quitte Calais à onze heures moins le quart,

Nous allons à Boulerque,

Vous venez d'où?

Mais il est dix heures et demie,

Route planning

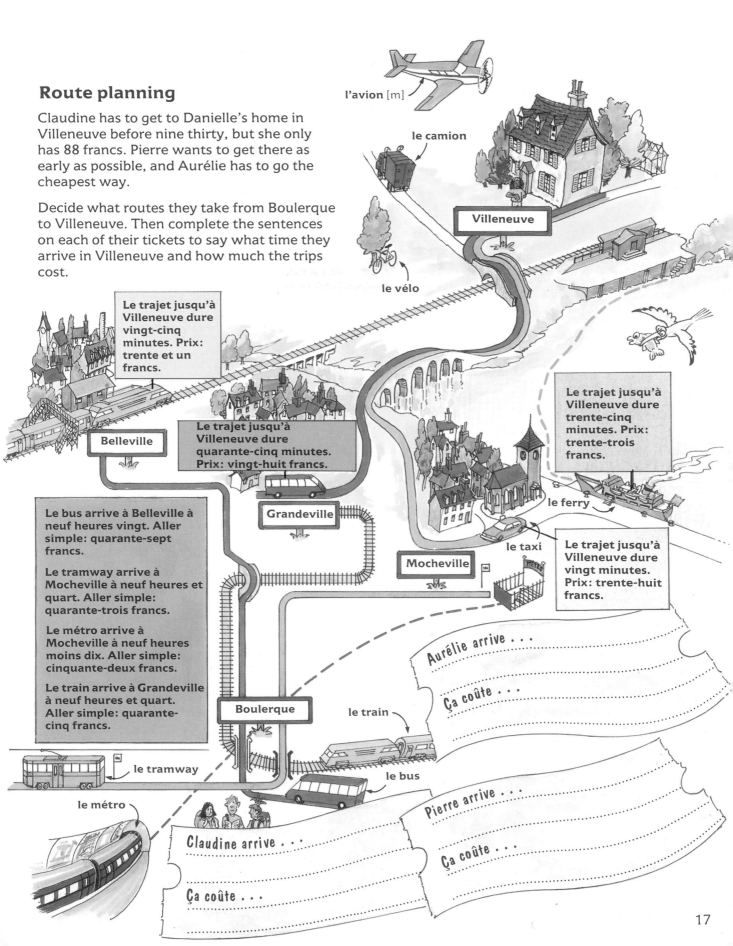

Claudine has to get to Danielle's home in Villeneuve before nine thirty, but she only has 88 francs. Pierre wants to get there as early as possible, and Aurélie has to go the cheapest way.

Decide what routes they take from Boulerque to Villeneuve. Then complete the sentences on each of their tickets to say what time they arrive in Villeneuve and how much the trips cost.

l'avion [m]

le camion

Villeneuve

le vélo

Le trajet jusqu'à Villeneuve dure vingt-cinq minutes. Prix: trente et un francs.

Belleville

Le trajet jusqu'à Villeneuve dure quarante-cinq minutes. Prix: vingt-huit francs.

Le trajet jusqu'à Villeneuve dure trente-cinq minutes. Prix: trente-trois francs.

Grandeville

le ferry

Le bus arrive à Belleville à neuf heures vingt. Aller simple: quarante-sept francs.

Le tramway arrive à Mocheville à neuf heures et quart. Aller simple: quarante-trois francs.

Le métro arrive à Mocheville à neuf heures moins dix. Aller simple: cinquante-deux francs.

Le train arrive à Grandeville à neuf heures et quart. Aller simple: quarante-cinq francs.

Mocheville

le taxi

Le trajet jusqu'à Villeneuve dure vingt minutes. Prix: trente-huit francs.

Aurélie arrive . . .

Ça coûte . . .

Boulerque

le train

le tramway

le bus

Pierre arrive . . .

Ça coûte . . .

le métro

Claudine arrive . . .

Ça coûte . . .

17

Finding your way

Here you will find puzzles for you to practice asking for and giving directions.

Word check

Here is the action word **prendre** (to take):

je prends	I take
tu prends	you take
il/elle prend	he/she/it takes
nous prenons	we take
vous prenez	you take
ils/elles prennent	they take

To tell someone to do something, you use the **tu** or **vous** word without **tu** or **vous**:

prends, prenez	take

Action words ending in "er" also lose the "s" from the **tu** word, for example:

va, allez	go
rentre, rentrez	go back/home

tourner	to turn
à gauche	(on the) left
à droite	(on the) right
tout droit	straight ahead
la première	first (turn)
la deuxième	second (turn)
la troisième	third (turn)
la rue	street
au bout de	at the end of
puis	then
devant	in front of
derrière	behind
à côté de	next to
entre	between
qui?	who?

Word search

The French for these words is hidden in the grid without **le**, **la**, **l'** or **les**. Circle the **les** nouns in red, the feminine ones in blue and the masculine ones in black.

sleeping bag	snake
trip	trucks
backpack	price
plate	table
swimsuit	bird
flag	planes
lunch	ferry
friends	street
bus	pigs
chair	subway

Locked in a maze

Danielle is locked in a maze. The directions below tell her where to go to find the key to the gate. (The animals she meets will not get in her way.) Can you draw a key on the maze to show where it is hidden?

Prends la première à gauche, puis la deuxième à droite. Va tout droit, puis prends la deuxième à droite. Tourne à gauche, puis prends la troisième à droite. Va tout droit, prends la première à droite et puis tourne à gauche. La clef est à côté de l'arbre au bout de la rue.

Once Danielle has the key, the animals will try to take it from her. If she picks it up and turns right, how can she then get back to the gate without bumping into them? Write the remaining eight directions for her. (Begin each one with **Prends**.)

1. ....
2. ....
3. ....
4. ....
5. ....
6. ....
7. ....
8. ....

A	I	D	F	E	R	R	Y	L	Y	E	P	A
S	T	R	M	W	H	C	O	C	H	O	N	S
E	G	A	H	C	U	O	C	E	D	C	A	S
R	À	P	R	I	M	É	T	R	O	V	T	I
P	C	E	Y	U	O	A	F	J	I	E	A	E
E	N	A	L	F	E	M	I	O	J	A	B	T
N	S	U	M	B	U	S	N	A	L	I	P	T
T	H	C	E	I	A	S	R	G	N	Y	R	E
M	A	I	L	L	O	T	D	E	B	A	I	N
T	D	É	J	E	U	N	E	R	X	M	X	O
D	S	O	D	À	C	A	S	D	D	I	G	U
O	I	S	E	A	U	C	H	A	I	S	E	B

18

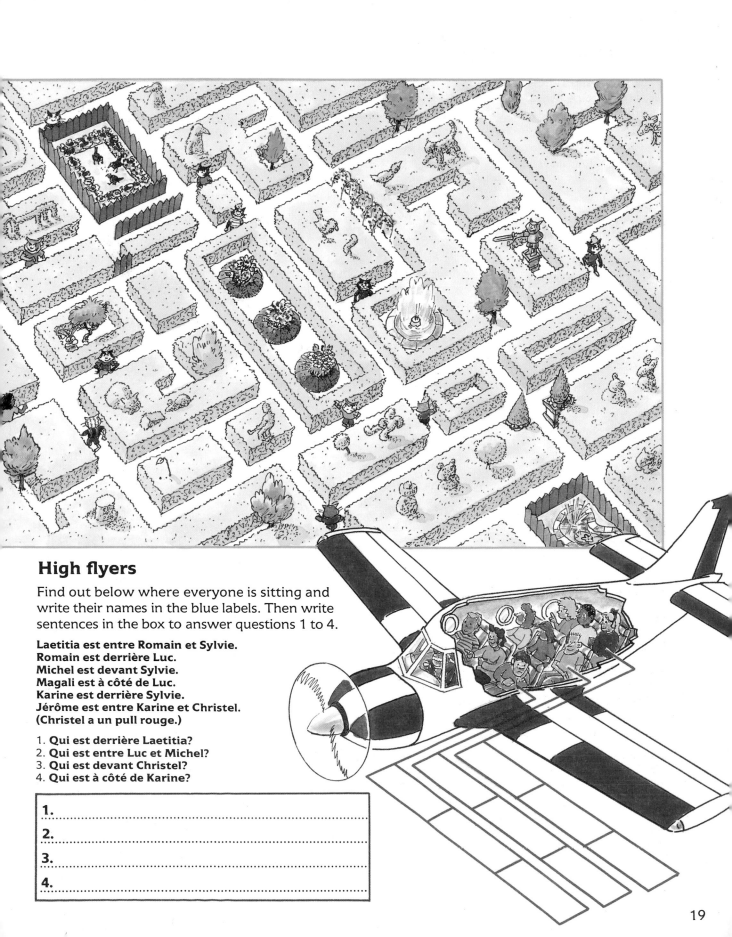

High flyers

Find out below where everyone is sitting and write their names in the blue labels. Then write sentences in the box to answer questions 1 to 4.

Laetitia est entre Romain et Sylvie.
Romain est derrière Luc.
Michel est devant Sylvie.
Magali est à côté de Luc.
Karine est derrière Sylvie.
Jérôme est entre Karine et Christel.
(Christel a un pull rouge.)

1. **Qui est derrière Laetitia?**
2. **Qui est entre Luc et Michel?**
3. **Qui est devant Christel?**
4. **Qui est à côté de Karine?**

1. ....
2. ....
3. ....
4. ....

Places to stay

These puzzles will help you say where things are and talk about where you are staying.

Word check

l'auberge de jeunesse [f]	youth hostel
le camping	campsite
l'hôtel [m]	hotel
à	to, at
à la maison	to/at the house
à l'hôtel	to/at the hotel

À turns into **au** in front of **le** words and **aux** in front of **les** words (you drop **le** and **les**):

au camping	to/at the campsite
aux États-Unis	to the United States
la chambre	room, bedroom
la salle de bain	bathroom
la porte	door
le lit	bed
le placard	cupboard, closet
la lampe	light
le miroir	mirror
le tapis	rug
le lavabo	sink
chercher	to look for
tant pis	too bad
excusez-moi	excuse me
demander (à quelqu'un)	to ask (someone)
pour aller à?	how do I get to?
vous avez?	do you have?
c'est complet	we're full
libre	free, available
seulement	only
il y a	there is/are
dans	in
sous	under
sur	on
en face de	across from
au-dessus de	above
en face de la chambre	across from the bedroom
à côté de l'hôtel	next to the hotel

De turns into **du** in front of **le** words and **des** in front of **les** words (you drop **le** and **les**):

au-dessus du lavabo	above the sink
à côté des chaises	next to the chairs

Packing for a trip

Claudine is packing. Check off the things on her list that she has already put in her backpack (they are shown in circles), then write sentences in the green box using **dans**, **sous** or **sur** to say where the other things on her list are. Begin each answer with the French for "Her . . . is/are."

une casserole
un verre
mon sac de couchage
mon maillot de bain
deux serviettes
ma carte
mon pantalon
ma jupe
deux pulls
ma chemise
mes trois livres
mon appareil-photo

A room for two

Read about Frédéric's room in the youth hostel, then finish his picture of it (shown on the right) by drawing in the six things he has left out.

Il y a une porte entre le lavabo et mon lit. Au-dessus du lavabo il y a un miroir. La lampe est au-dessus de la table. La table est entre le lavabo et le placard. Il y a une chaise entre mon lit et le lit de Guillaume. Il y a un tapis devant la porte.

This is Guillaume's description of the room but it is not complete. Can you fill in the missing words?

Le lavabo est entre la porte et.........................Le miroir est au-dessus.........................Le placard est.........................la table. Le lit de Frédéric est.........................la porte. La chaise est.........................les deux lits.

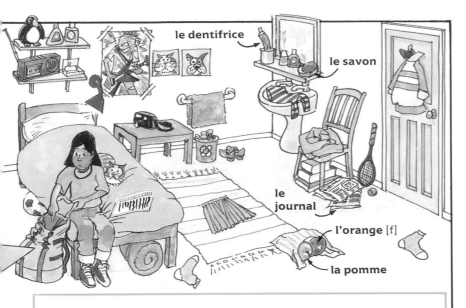

le dentifrice

le savon

le journal

l'orange [f]

la pomme

A place for shelter

Aurélie and Margot are on a camping trip and it hasn't stopped raining. Can you unscramble this story to find out what they do? Put the numbers of each part of the story in the right order in the boxes at the bottom of the page.

1. **Elles arrivent à l'hôtel Bon Marché à neuf heures moins le quart.**

2. **"Prenez la première à gauche, allez tout droit, puis tournez à droite. L'auberge de jeunesse est au bout de la rue."**

3. **"Oui. J'ai une chambre avec une salle de bain."**

4. **Mais elles ont seulement quatre-vingt-dix francs! Tant pis! Elles rentrent au camping.**

5. **"Non, c'est complet." Elles quittent l'auberge de jeunesse et cherchent un hôtel.**

6. **Aurélie demande à quelqu'un: "Excusez-moi, Monsieur. Pour aller à l'auberge de jeunesse, s'il vous plaît?"**

7. **"Quatre-vingt-quatorze francs."**

8. **Elles arrivent à l'auberge de jeunesse. "Vous avez deux lits?" demande Aurélie.**

9. **"Vous avez une chambre?" demandent-elles.**

10. **Aurélie et Margot quittent le camping à huit heures dix. Elles cherchent l'auberge de jeunesse.**

11. **"C'est combien?"**

1. ....

2. ....

3. ....

4. ....

5. ....

6. ....

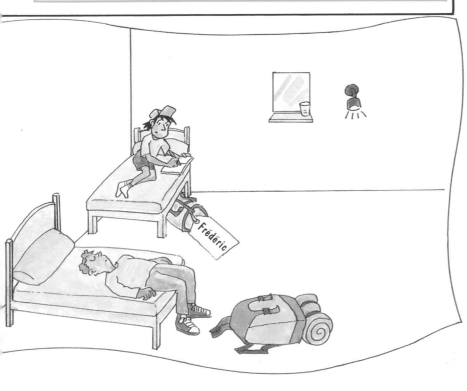

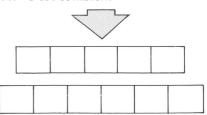

⬇

Around town

Here you can practice the French you need for visiting towns and cities.

Word check

la gare	station
la station de métro	subway station
la gare routière	bus station
l'arrêt d'autobus [m]	bus stop
la banque	bank
le marché	market
l'office du tourisme [m]	tourist office
le jardin public	park
la poste	post office
la station-service	gas station
les toilettes (publiques) [f]	(public) washroom
la cabine téléphonique	phone booth
le café	café
le restaurant	restaurant
la cathédrale	cathedral
le château	castle
le musée	museum
la piscine	swimming pool
le cinéma	movie theater
le magasin	store
la pharmacie	pharmacy
le supermarché	supermarket
le timbre	stamp
le traveller's chèque	traveler's check
la crème solaire	sun-tan lotion
l'essence [f]	gasoline
le passeport	passport
la visite	tour, visit
je voudrais	I would like
commencer	to start, to begin
changer	to change, to cash (a traveler's check)
là-bas	over there
votre	your (for an adult you don't know well)
où est/sont?	where is/are?

Matchmaking

Can you pair off the pieces of French below to make seven conversations? Put a number and a letter next to the name of the place where you might hear people saying these things.

1. **Un timbre, s'il vous plaît.**
2. **Un aller-retour pour Boulerque, s'il vous plaît.**
3. **Excusez-moi, je cherche le dentifrice.**
4. **Un jus d'orange, s'il vous plaît.**
5. **Je voudrais changer un traveller's chèque, s'il vous plaît.**
6. **La visite commence à neuf heures?**
7. **Où est le musée?**

A. **Soixante-six francs, s'il vous plaît. Le train quitte Calais à neuf heures cinq.**
B. **Vous avez votre passeport?**
C. **Non, à dix heures et demie.**
D. **Devant le château.**
E. **Grand ou petit?**
F. **Là-bas, à côté du savon.**
G. **Pour la France?**

La banque:		
La gare:		
La poste:		

Le château:		
L'office du tourisme:		
Le supermarché:		
Le café:		

Scrambled French

Can you unscramble these words to find the names of five things and five places where you can get them? Write the names of the things next to their numbers in the purple box, and then put the right place next to each one. (Don't forget **le**, **la**, **l'** or **les**.)

	Things	Places
1.	GROANELESS	EALRAG
2.	ASMELLIEROACÈR	RATTIESNOCLAVISE
3.	BRILTEEM	CRAMHÉEL
4.	REALPLIMSELL	STEAPLO
5.	SNEECLES	CRAMPIEHALA

1.	
2.	
3.	
4.	
5.	

A break in Boulerque

Here is what Debbie was told when she went to the Boulerque tourist office. Can you decide what her questions were and write them in the box on the right?

1. **Tournez à gauche, puis prenez la deuxième à droite. Elle est au bout de la rue.**
2. **Tournez à droite, puis prenez la deuxième à droite.**
3. **À côté de la station de métro.**
4. **En face de la cathédrale.**

1. ....
2. ....
3. ....
4. ....

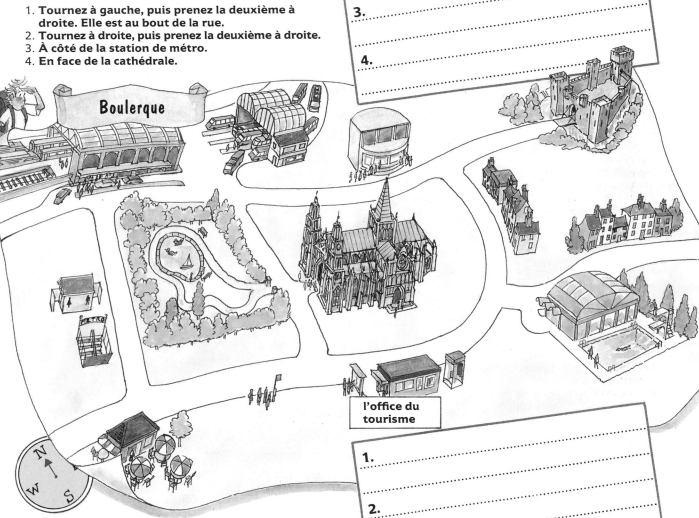

Boulerque

l'office du tourisme

Here are eight things Bill needs to ask when he is looking for somewhere to stay. Can you put them into French for him?

1. How do I get to the campsite, please?
2. Where is the youth hostel, please?
3. Do you have a bed?
4. How do I get to the hotel, please?
5. Do you have a room?
6. How much is it?
7. Excuse me, I would like to cash a traveler's check.
8. Where is the washroom?

1. ....
2. ....
3. ....
4. ....
5. ....
6. ....
7. ....
8. ....

23

On vacation

These puzzles are all about organizing your vacation activities.

Word check

Here is the action word **faire** (to do, to make):

je fais	I do
tu fais	you do
il/elle fait	he/she/it does
nous faisons	we do
vous faites	you do
ils/elles font	they do

Faire is used to talk about activities:

faire du ski	to go skiing
faire ...	to go ...
du ski nautique	waterskiing
de la planche à voile	windsurfing
du canoë	canoeing
du patin à glace	ice-skating
de la randonnée	walking (in the country)
du vélo	cycling
du cheval	horseback riding

le canoë	canoe
des skis [m]	(some) skis
le forfait	ski pass
les remontées mécaniques [f]	ski lifts
la patinoire	ice rink
être/aller en vacances	to be/go on vacation
nager	to swim
aller à la pêche	to go fishing
visiter	to visit (a place)
louer	to rent
la mer	sea
la plage	beach
la campagne	countryside
la montagne	mountains
les grottes [f]	caves
les ruines [f]	ruins
le parc d'attractions	amusement park
la rivière	river
la discothèque	disco
l'exposition [f]	exhibition
la peinture	painting
le matin	(in the) morning
le soir	(in the) evening

Pierre's day on the island ...

Number Pierre's plans for the day (listed below) from one to eight to show the order he does everything in. Then mark on the map the route he takes around the island. (He goes the shortest way.)

Je vais à la discothèque à neuf heures.
Je fais du canoë sur la rivière à quatre heures.
Je visite le parc d'attractions à onze heures vingt.
Le soir, je rentre au camping à onze heures et demie.
Je fais de la planche à voile à dix heures moins le quart.
Le matin, je quitte le camping à neuf heures.
Je visite les grottes à deux heures.
Je vais au restaurant à une heure.

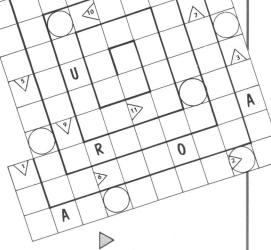

Vacation cube

Below are some things you might do on vacation. Complete the grid by writing around it the names of the places where you can do these things. (The numbers show where to start each answer.) Then see what you can spell in French with the circled letters and write it in the space provided. (Don't forget **le**, **la**, **l'** or **les**.)

1. **Faire de la randonnée.**
2. **Faire du ski nautique.**
3. **Aller à la pêche.**
4. **Acheter une pomme.**
5. **Prendre un train.**
6. **Faire du ski.**
7. **Nager.**
8. **Changer un traveller's chèque.**
9. **Prendre un bus.**
10. **Aller à une exposition.**
11. **Faire du patin à glace.**

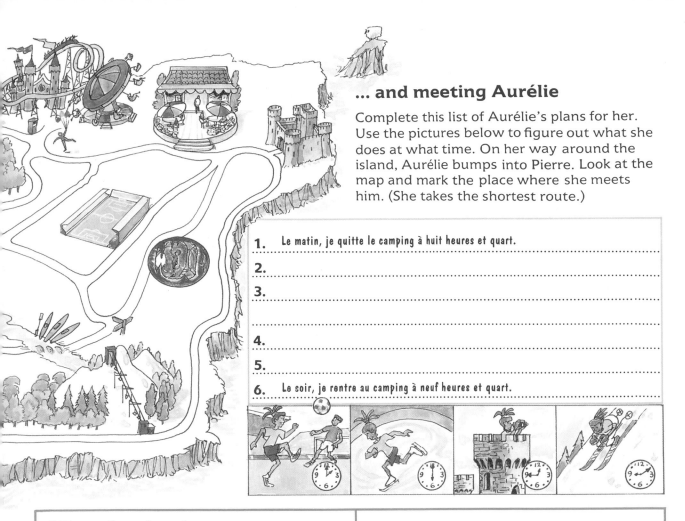

... and meeting Aurélie

Complete this list of Aurélie's plans for her. Use the pictures below to figure out what she does at what time. On her way around the island, Aurélie bumps into Pierre. Look at the map and mark the place where she meets him. (She takes the shortest route.)

1. Le matin, je quitte le camping à huit heures et quart.
2.
3.
4.
5.
6. Le soir, je rentre au camping à neuf heures et quart.

All set for the slopes

Read about Céline's vacation, then write complete sentences in French to answer the seven questions below.

Céline est en vacances à Neigeville. Elle fait du ski. Le matin, elle quitte l'auberge de jeunesse et va à l'office du tourisme: "Bonjour, Monsieur. Je voudrais un forfait, s'il vous plaît. C'est combien?" "Quatre-vingt-dix francs."

Elle cherche quatre-vingt-dix francs et demande: "Je voudrais louer des skis. Où est le magasin, s'il vous plaît?" "En face de la patinoire."

Céline loue des skis et arrive aux remontées mécaniques à dix heures. Elle cherche son forfait. Mais il est sur la table à l'office du tourisme!

1. Where is Céline on vacation?
2. How much does a ski pass cost?
3. What does Céline rent?
4. Where is the store for renting skis?
5. What time does Céline arrive at the ski lifts?
6. What does she do when she gets to the lifts?
7. Where is Céline's ski pass?

1.
2.
3.
4.
5.
6.
7.

Round-up

These two pages practice a lot of the French that you have already used in this book.

Crossword

Fill in the crossword using the clues below. To get the right answers, think of French words that would fit into the blanks. (The words you will need have all been used in this book.) Don't forget the French for "a" or "the."

Across

1. **Il y a un lavabo dans ...** (2, 5, 2, 4)
3. **Pierre est ... et blond.** (See page 3.) (5)
4. **"Bonjour, ... "** (6)
8. **Une pharmacie est ...** (2, 7)
11. **" ... de jus d'orange, s'il vous plaît."** (2, 5)
13. **Le matin, tu vas à ...** (1, 5)
15. **"..., ça va bien."** (3)
17. **Le drapeau de la France est bleu, ... et rouge** (5)
18. **"Prenez la première à gauche. La gare est au bout de ... "** (2, 3)

Down

1. **Tu prends le bus à ...** (2, 4, 8)
2. **Tu achètes ... au supermarché.** (2, 10)
5. **Le train quitte la gare dans trois ...** (7)
6. **Tu prends un train à ...** (2, 4)
7. **Tu fais du patin à glace à ...** (2, 9)
9. **Il y a ... minutes dans une heure.** (8)
10. **Claudine fait du vélo. ... est blanc.** (3, 4)
12. **... baleines nagent dans la mer.** (3)
14. **Un journal est ... et blanc** (4)
16. **Pierre a dix ans. ... vient de Lyon.** (2)

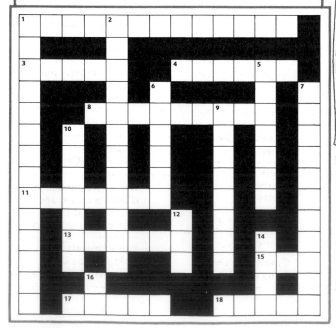

What are they all doing?

Read these descriptions of five people, then write sentences in the black box to say what each one is doing in the picture below.

1. **Hélène est grande et brune. Elle a un maillot de bain vert.**
2. **Hervé est petit et blond. Il a un pantalon noir.**
3. **Didier est grand et blond. Il a un pull bleu.**
4. **Fabrice est petit et brun. Il a une chemise blanche.**
5. **Gabrielle est petite et blonde. Elle a un maillot de bain rouge.**

1. ....
2. ....
3. ....
4. ....
5. ....

A ghostly encounter

Can you complete this story about Debbie and Bill's visit to the famous ruins of Château Sinistre? Put a number next to each piece of French in the gray box below to show which blank it fits into.

*Debbie and Bill wanted to find their way to the ruins' underground caves, so they went up to a tall blond-haired man and Debbie asked, "...**1**..." "...**2**...," the strange man replied, adjusting his dusty green shirt. He had realized she wasn't French, so he asked her, "...**3**..." "...**4**...," Debbie answered.*

*"...**5**...," the man asked them. They told him their names and asked him his: "...**6**..." "...**7**...," he replied. Émile wanted to know where they were staying: "...**8**..." Bill shook his head and replied, "...**9**..."*

*Then all of a sudden Émile disappeared through a stone door, waving and calling "...**10**..." At that moment the castle caretaker arrived. "...**11**...," he said, pointing at his watch – the ruins were about to close.*

*As the caretaker was leading the children down Fantôme steps, Bill asked who used to live in the castle. "...**12**...," the caretaker replied. The children looked at each other, and Debbie asked the caretaker what Émile had looked like. He replied, "...**13**..."*

Picture pitfalls

Margot's description of this picture has a lot of mistakes in it. Can you rewrite it, changing the things that are wrong?

Il est onze heures dix. Frédéric est blond et il a un pantalon noir. Isabelle est petite et brune. Elle a un pantalon blanc et son sac à dos est bleu. Il y a cinq tentes au camping. Une voiture rouge quitte la gare. Devant la gare il y a un lac. Il y a neuf vaches et à côté du lac il y a un mouton. Sur le lac une fille fait du ski nautique.

....

....

....

....

....

....

....

....

....

....

....

....

Non, au camping.		**Tu viens d'où?**
Comment vous vous appelez?		**Excusez-moi, pour aller aux grottes, s'il vous plaît?**
Il est six heures,		**Au revoir!**
Je m'appelle Émile Sinistre,		**Je viens des États-Unis.**
Vous êtes à l'auberge de jeunesse?		**Il y a une peinture d'Émile au musée. Il est grand avec une chemise verte.**
Émile Sinistre, le grand-père de mon grand-père,		**Allez tout droit, puis prenez la première à gauche,**
Comment vous vous appelez?		

Answers to puzzles

p.2-3

Putting words in their mouths

A. Au revoir.
B. Pas très bien.
C. Bonsoir, Monsieur.
D. Ça va bien.
E. Salut.
F. Bonjour, Madame.
G. Au revoir.

What are their names?

A. Comment elle s'appelle?
B. Je m'appelle Aurélie.
C. Il s'appelle Pierre.
D. Ils s'appellent Danielle et Frédéric.

Wordspinner

The ten greetings or names of things are:

bonsoir	le chien
la glace	ça va?
au revoir	la maison
le soleil	salut
bonjour	le crabe

p.4-5

Lost for words

1. C   2. C   3. A

4. B   5. A

Word search

1. le crabe	8. le soleil
2. la voiture	9. le stylo
3. le chat	10. la fille
4. la montre	11. la glace
5. le chien	12. la maison
6. le parasol	13. l'église
7. la carte	14. la clef

Lost and found

The six things that Pierre picks up:

1. l'appareil-photo
2. la clef
3. la carte
4. le livre
5. le stylo
6. la montre

p.6-7

How old are they?

A. Tu as huit ans.
B. Nous avons douze ans.
C. Ils ont douze ans.
D. Vous avez onze ans.
E. Il a neuf ans.

1. Il a treize ans.
2. Elle a dix ans.
3. Nous avons onze ans.
4. J'ai .... ans.

Island hoppers

The thing Frédéric left off his list was:

un chat

The three islands he visited were:

l'Île Blanche
l'Île Rouge
l'Île Jaune

The thing Claudine left off her list was:

une maison

The three islands she visited were:

l'Île Bleue
l'Île Verte
l'Île Jaune

What's in the dots?

une clef OR la clef

p.8-9

Around the world

A. le pays de Galles
B. l'Écosse
C. la Norvège
D. l'Angleterre
E. les Pays-Bas
F. l'Espagne
G. la France
H. l'Allemagne
I. l'Autriche
J. la Corse

1. Il vient du pays de Galles.
2. Il vient d'Angleterre.
3. Ils viennent de France.
4. Elle vient des Pays-Bas.
5. Ils viennent d'Allemagne.
6. Ils viennent de Norvège.
7. Elle vient d'Italie.
8. Elles viennent d'Espagne.

Slot machine

Nous venons d'Italie.
Je viens de France.
Vous venez d'Écosse.
Tu viens du Portugal.
Ils viennent du Danemark.

French crossword

p.10-11

Family connections

A. Jean
B. Françoise
C. Bernadette
D. Francine
E. Jacques
F. Guy
G. Marc
H. Frédéric
I. Dominique
J. Monique

1. Jean et Françoise sont les parents de Guy OR Les parents de Guy sont Jean et Françoise.
2. Jean est le grand-père de Claudine OR Le grand-père de Claudine est Jean.
3. Bernadette est la mère de Dominique OR La mère de Dominique est Bernadette.
4. Guy est l'oncle de Marc OR L'oncle de Marc est Guy.

Word cross

an aunt

Scrambled letters

The writing on the envelopes says:

1. mon père
2. ma tante
3. mes grands-parents
4. mon cousin

Dominique did not write to:

sa mère
son oncle
son frère
ses cousines

Spot the mistakes

1. Bernadette **est ma** mère.
2. Guy **est mon** oncle.
3. Monique **et** Claudine sont mes **cousines**.
4. Jean et Françoise **sont mes** grands-parents.
5. Je **suis** le **frère** de Dominique.
6. Monique et Claudine **sont les** soeurs de Frédéric.
7. Frédéric est **mon cousin**.

p.12-13

Odd ones out

A. Flavien
B. Margot
C. Marc
D. Isabelle
E. Nathalie
F. Céline
G. Guillaume
H. Sylvain
I. Claire
J. Yves

The descriptions Aurélie has left out are:
Elle est petite et blonde.
Il est grand et brun.

Clipped sentences

1. Il vient de France.
2. J'ai onze ans.
3. Elle s'appelle Dominique.
4. Ça va bien.
5. Elles s'appellent Claudine et Danielle.
6. Nous venons de Chine.
7. Ils s'appellent Pierre et Aurélie.
8. Je viens d'Espagne.

p.14-15

Clockwork

Here are the completed clockfaces:

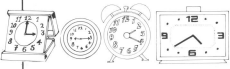

1. Il est onze heures moins le quart.
2. Il est dix heures et quart.
3. Il est sept heures moins dix.
4. Il est une heure et demie.
5. Il est quatre heures cinq.

Word circle

1. je rentre
2. tu as
3. nous arrivons
4. vous venez
5. j'ai
6. j'arrive
7. il est
8. elle joue
9. tu es
10. nous quittons
11. il a
12. ils jouent

p.16-17

Time travelers

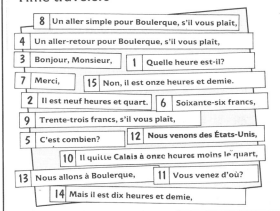

8   Un aller simple pour Boulerque, s'il vous plaît,
4   Un aller-retour pour Boulerque, s'il vous plaît,
3   Bonjour, Monsieur,   1   Quelle heure est-il?
7   Merci,   15   Non, il est onze heures et demie.
2   Il est neuf heures et quart.   6   Soixante-six francs,
9   Trente-trois francs, s'il vous plaît,
5   C'est combien?   12   Nous venons des États-Unis,
10   Il quitte Calais à onze heures le quart.
13   Nous allons à Boulerque,   11   Vous venez d'où?
14   Mais il est dix heures et demie,

Postcard to a pen pal

Dear Vicky,
How are you? My name is Danielle and I am twelve (years old). I come from France. I have one sister and a cat. My sister's name is Aline. She is nine (years old). I am tall and dark, and my sister is short and dark. How old are you?

Love,
Danielle

Chère Danielle,
Je m'appelle Vicky. J'ai onze ans et je viens des États-Unis. Je suis grande et blonde. J'ai un frère. Il s'appelle Nick et il a treize ans. J'ai deux soeurs. Elles s'appellent Alison et Lucy. Elles ont sept ans.

Grosses bises,
Vicky

The piece of French spelled out in the gray section means:

A day in the life

The picture numbers are (in the right order):
9, 2, 8, 5, 4.

Here is the story of Philippe's day:

Philippe vient de Paris. Il a douze ans, il est grand et brun. Il a deux frères et une soeur.
Il quitte la maison à sept heures et quart.
Il arrive à l'école à huit heures cinq. (Après le déjeuner,) il joue au football avec son amie. Son amie est grande et brune.
Il quitte l'école à quatre heures moins le quart.

Route planning

Aurélie arrive (à Villeneuve) à dix heures. Ça coûte soixante-treize francs.

Claudine arrive (à Villeneuve) à neuf heures vingt-cinq. Ça coûte quatre-vingt-cinq francs.

Pierre arrive (à Villeneuve) à neuf heures dix. Ça coûte quatre-vingt-dix francs.

p.18-19

Locked in a maze

1. Prends la première à droite.
2. Prends la deuxième à droite.
3. Prends la première à gauche.
4. Prends la deuxième à gauche.
5. Prends la première à gauche.
6. Prends la troisième à gauche.
7. Prends la troisième à gauche.
8. Prends la première à droite.

The picture below shows where the key is hidden:

Word search

   shows the red circles
   shows the blue circles

A	I	D	F	E	R	R	Y	L	Y	E	P	A
S	T	R	M	W	H	C	O	C	H	O	N	S
E	G	A	H	C	U	O	C	E	D	C	A	S
R	A	P	R	I	M	Ê	T	R	O	V	T	I
P	C	E	R	U	O	A	F	J	E	A	E	T
E	N	L	F	E	M	I	G	J	A	B	T	
N	S	U	M	B	U	S	N	A	L	I	P	T
T	H	C	E	I	A	S	R	G	N	Y	R	E
M	A	I	L	L	O	T	D	E	B	A	I	N
T	D	É	J	E	U	N	E	R	C	M	X	O.
D	S	O	D	A	C	A	S	D	I	G	U	S
O	I	S	E	A	U	C	H	A	I	S	E	B

High flyers

Karine	Jérôme	Christel
Sylvie	Laetitia	Romain
Michel	Magali	Luc

1. Jérôme est derrière Laetitia.
2. Magali est entre Luc et Michel.
3. Romain est devant Christel.
4. Jérôme est à côté de Karine.

p.20-21

Packing for a trip

The things on Claudine's list that you should have checked off are:
une casserole, une verre, deux serviettes, ma carte, mon pantalon, deux pulls.

Son sac de couchage est sous le lit.
Son maillot de bain est dans le lavabo.
Sa jupe est sur le tapis.

Sa chemise est sur la chaise.
Ses (trois) livres sont sous la chaise.
Son appareil-photo est sur la table.

A room for two

This picture shows the missing things:

Le lavabo est entre la porte et la table. Le miroir est au-dessus du lavabo. Le placard est à côté de la table. Le lit de Frédéric est à côté de la porte. La chaise est entre les deux lits.

A place for shelter

The numbers in the right order are:
10, 6, 2, 8, 5, 1, 9, 3, 11, 7, 4.

p.22-23

Matchmaking

La banque: 5 B
La gare: 2 A
La poste: 1 G
Le château: 6 C

L'office du
tourisme: 7 D
Le supermarché: 3 F
Le café: 4 E

Scrambled French

1. les oranges
2. la crème solaire
3. le timbre
4. l'aller simple
5. l'essence

le marché
la pharmacie
la poste
la gare
la station-
service

A break in Boulerque

1. Pour aller à la gare (s'il vous plaît)? OR Où est la gare (s'il vous plaît)?
2. Pour aller au château (s'il vous plaît)? OR Où est le château (s'il vous plaît)?
3. Où sont les toilettes publiques (s'il vous plaît)?
4. Où est le jardin public (s'il vous plaît)?

The eight things Bill says are:

1. Pour aller au camping, s'il vous plaît?
2. Où est l'auberge de jeunesse, s'il vous plaît?
3. Vous avez un lit?
4. Pour aller à l'hôtel, s'il vous plaît?
5. Vous avez une chambre?
6. C'est combien?
7. Excusez-moi, je voudrais changer un traveller's chèque.
8. Où sont les toilettes?

p.24-25

Pierre's day on the island...

7. Je vais à la discothèque à neuf heures.
6. Je fais du canoë sur la rivière à quatre heures.
3. Je visite le parc d'attractions à onze heures vingt.
8. Le soir, je rentre au camping à onze heures et demie.
2. Je fais de la planche à voile à dix heures moins le quart.
1. Le matin, je quitte le camping à neuf heures.
5. Je visite les grottes à deux heures.
4. Je vais au restaurant à une heure.

... and meeting Aurélie

1. Le matin, je quitte le camping à huit heures et quart.
2. Je fais du ski à neuf heures dix OR À neuf heures dix, je fais du ski.
3. Je visite le château à une heure moins le quart OR À une heure moins le quart, je visite le château.
4. Je joue au football à deux heures OR À deux heures, je joue au football.
5. Je fais du patin à glace à six heures OR À six heures, je fais du patin à glace.
6. Le soir, je rentre au camping à neuf heures et quart.

Here you can see Pierre's route and the place where he meets Aurélie:

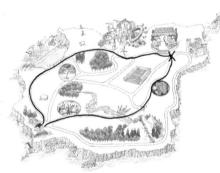

Vacation cube

1. la campagne
2. le lac
3. la rivière
4. le marché
5. la gare
6. la montagne
7. la mer
8. la banque
9. l'arrêt d'autobus
10. le musée
11. la patinoire

The word you can spell with the circled letters is:

la plage

All set for the slopes

1. Céline est (en vacances) à Neigeville OR Elle est (en vacances) à Neigeville.
2. Ça coûte quatre-vingt-dix francs.
3. Céline loue des skis OR Elle loue des skis.

4. Le magasin est en face de la patinoire OR Il est en face de la patinoire.
5. Céline arrive (aux remontées mécaniques) à dix heures OR Elle arrive (aux remontées mécaniques) à dix heures.
6. Céline cherche son forfait OR Elle cherche son forfait.
7. Son forfait est (sur la table) à l'office du tourisme OR Le forfait de Céline est (sur la table) à l'office du tourisme OR Il est (sur la table) à l'office du tourisme.

p.26-27

Crossword

What are they all doing?

1. Hélène (OR Elle) fait de la planche à voile.
2. Hervé (OR Il) fait du vélo.
3. Didier (OR Il) joue au football.
4. Fabrice (OR Il) fait du cheval.
5. Gabrielle (OR Elle) nage.

Picture pitfalls

Il est onze heures **moins** dix. Frédéric est **brun** et il a un pantalon **bleu**. Isabelle est **grande** et brune. Elle a un pantalon **noir** et son sac à dos est **vert**. Il y a **six** tentes au camping. **Un train jaune** quitte la gare. **Derrière** la gare il y a un lac (OR Devant la gare il y a **une rue/un camping**). Il y a **huit** vaches et à côté du lac il y a un **cheval**. Sur le lac une fille fait **de la planche à voile**.

A ghostly encounter

9	Non, au camping.	3	Tu viens d'où?
5 (6)	Comment vous vous appelez?	1	Excusez-moi, pour aller aux grottes, s'il vous plaît?
11	Il est six heures,	10	Au revoir!
7	Je m'appelle Émile Sinistre,	4	Je viens des États-Unis.
8	Vous êtes à l'auberge de jeunesse?	13	Il y a une peinture d'Émile au musée. Il est grand avec une chemise verte.
12	Émile Sinistre, le grand-père de mon grand-père,		
6 (5)	Comment vous vous appelez?	2	Allez tout droit, puis prenez la première à gauche,

French–English word list

Here you can find the French words used in this book with their English meanings. The [m] and [f] after a word show whether it is masculine or feminine.

Most nouns just add an "s" when they turn into **les** words (**le chat** – cat, **les chats** – cats). Some work differently, and they are shown here with their **les** words in parentheses.

After most masculine describing words you can see in parentheses the letters you can add to make them feminine. For those with a very different feminine word, both words are shown.

à	to, at
acheter	to buy
à côté de	next to
à droite	(on the) right
à gauche	(on the) left
l'Allemagne [f]	Germany
aller	to go
aller à la pêche	to go fishing
aller en vacances	to go on vacation
l'aller-retour [m] (les aller-retour)	round trip (ticket)
l'aller simple [m] (les allers simples)	one way (ticket)
l'ami [m], l'amie [f]	friend
l'Angleterre [f]	England
l'appareil-photo [m] (les appareils-photos)	camera
après	after
l'arbre [m]	tree
l'arrêt d'autobus [m]	bus stop
arriver	to arrive
l'assiette [f]	plate
l'auberge de jeunesse [f]	youth hostel
au bout de	at the end of
au-dessus de	above
au revoir	goodbye
l'Australie [f]	Australia
l'Autriche [f]	Austria
avec	with
l'avion [m]	plane
avoir	to have
la baleine	whale
la banque	bank
beau [m], belle [f]	pretty, beautiful
la Belgique	Belgium
blanc(he)	white
bleu(e)	blue
blond(e)	blond
bonjour	hello, good morning/afternoon
bon marché	cheap
bonsoir	good evening
brun(e)	dark
le bus (les bus)	bus
la cabine téléphonique	phone booth
ça coûte	it/that costs

le café	café
le camion	truck
la campagne	countryside
le camping	campsite
le canoë	canoe
la carte	map
la casserole	saucepan
la cathédrale	cathedral
ça va?	how are you?, are you all right?
ça va bien	fine
cent	a hundred
c'est combien?	how much is it/that?
c'est complet	we're full
la chaise	chair
la chambre	room, bedroom
changer	to change, to cash (a traveler's check)
le chat	cat
le château (les châteaux)	castle
la chemise	shirt
cher [m], chère [f]	dear
chercher	to look for
le cheval (les chevaux)	horse
le chien	dog
la Chine	China
le cinéma	movie theater
cinq	five
cinquante	fifty
la clef	key
le cochon	pig
commencer	to start, to begin
comment il/elle s'appelle?	what is his/her name?
comment ils/elles s'appellent?	what are their names?
comment tu t'appelles?	what is your name?
comment vous vous appelez?	what is your name?
la Corse	Corsica
le cousin, la cousine	cousin
le crabe	crab
la crème solaire	suntan lotion
le Danemark	Denmark
dans	in
de	from, of
le déjeuner	dinner
demander (à quelqu'un)	to ask (someone)
le dentifrice	toothpaste
derrière	behind
deux	two
deuxième	second
devant	in front of
la discothèque	disco
dix	ten
dix-huit	eighteen
dix-neuf	nineteen
dix-sept	seventeen
d'où?	where ... from?
douze	twelve
le drapeau (les drapeaux)	flag
l'école [f]	school
l'Écosse [f]	Scotland
l'église [f]	church
elle	she, it

elles	they
en face de	across from
entre	between
l'Espagne [f]	Spain
l'essence [f]	gasoline
et	and
les États-Unis [m]	the United States
et demie	half past
et quart	a quarter after
être	to be
être en vacances	to go on vacation
excusez-moi	excuse me
l'exposition [f]	exhibition
faire	to make/do
faire de la planche à voile	to go windsurfing
faire de la randonnée	to go walking (in the country)
faire du canoë	to go canoeing
faire du cheval	to go horseback riding
faire du patin à glace	to go ice-skating
faire du ski	to go skiing
faire du ski nautique	to go waterskiing
faire du vélo	to go cycling
la famille	family
le fantôme	ghost
la femme	wife, woman
le ferry	ferry
la fille	girl
la fleur	flower
le forfait	ski pass
la fourchette	fork
le franc	franc
la France	France
le frère	brother
la gare	station
la gare routière	bus station
la glace	ice cream
grand(e)	big
la grand-mère	grandmother
le grand-père	grandfather
les grands-parents [m]	grandparents
grosses bises	love (to end a letter)
les grottes [f]	caves
le hérisson	hedgehog
l'heure [f]	hour
l'hôtel [m]	hotel
huit	eight
il	he, it
il/elle s'appelle	his/her name is
il est ... heure(s)	it is ... o'clock
l'île [f]	island
ils	they
ils/elles s'appellent	their names are
ils viennent d'où?	where do they come from?
il y a	there is/are
l'Irlande [f]	Ireland
l'Italie [f]	Italy
j'ai dix ans	I am ten (years old)
le jardin public	park

jaune	yellow
je	I
je m'appelle	My name is
je voudrais	I would like
jouer (au football)	to play (soccer)
le journal (les journaux)	newspaper
la jupe	skirt
le jus d'orange	orange juice
là-bas	over there
le lac	lake
la lampe	light
le lapin	rabbit
le lavabo	sink
le/la/l'/les	the
libre	free, available
le lit	bed
le livre	book
louer	to rent
le Luxembourg	Luxembourg
Madame	Mrs.
le magasin	store
le maillot de bain (les maillots de bain)	swimsuit
mais	but
la maison	house
le marché	market
le mari	husband
le matin	(in the) morning
la mer	sea
merci	thank you
la mère	mother
le métro	subway
le midi	noon
la minute	minute
le miroir	mirror
moche	ugly
moins le quart	a quarter to
mon/ma/mes	my
Monsieur	Mr.
la montagne	mountains
la montre	watch
le mouton	sheep
le musée	museum
nager	to swim
la neige	snow
neuf	nine
neuf [m], neuve [f]	new
noir(e)	black
non	no
la Norvège	Norway
nous	we
l'office du tourisme [m]	tourist office
l'oiseau [m] (les oiseaux)	bird
l'oncle [m]	uncle
onze	eleven
l'orange [f]	orange
ou	or
où	where
où est/sont?	where is/are?
oui	yes
le pantalon	pants
le papillon	butterfly
le parasol	beach umbrella
le parc d'attractions	amusement park
les parents [m]	parents
le passeport	passport

pas très bien	not very well
la patinoire	ice rink
les Pays-Bas [m]	the Netherlands
le pays de Galles	Wales
la peinture	painting
le père	father
petit(e)	small
la pharmacie	drugstore, pharmacy
la piscine	swimming pool
le placard	cupboard, closet
la plage	beach
la pomme	apple
le pont	bridge
la porte	door
le Portugal	Portugal
la poste	post office
pour	for, to
pour aller à?	how do I get to?
première	first
prendre	to take
le prix (les prix)	price
puis	then
le pull	sweater, pullover
quarante	forty
quatorze	fourteen
quatre	four
quatre-vingt-dix	ninety
quatre-vingt-onze	ninety-one
quatre-vingts	eighty
quatre-vingt-un	eighty-one
quel âge as-tu?	how old are you?
quelle heure est-il?	what time is it?
qui?	who?
quinze	fifteen
quitter	to leave
les remontées mécaniques [f]	ski lifts
rentrer	to go back (home)
le restaurant	restaurant
la rivière	river
la robe	dress
rouge	red
la rue	street
les ruines [f]	ruins
le sac à dos (les sacs à dos)	backpack
le sac de couchage (les sacs de couchage)	sleeping bag
la salade	salad
la salle de bain	bathroom
salut	hi, hello, bye
la Sardaigne	Sardinia
la saucisse	sausage
le savon	soap
seize	sixteen
le sentier	path
sept	seven
le serpent	snake
la serviette	towel
seulement	only
la Sicile	Sicily
s'il vous plaît	please
sinistre	sinister
six	six
des skis [m]	skis
la soeur	sister
le soir	evening
soixante	sixty
soixante-dix	seventy
soixante et onze	seventy-one
le soleil	sun
son/sa/ses	his, her

la souris (les souris)	mouse
sous	under
la station de métro	subway station
la station-service	gas station
le stylo	pen
la Suisse	Switzerland
le supermarché	supermarket
sur	on
la table	table
la tante	aunt
tant pis	too bad
le tapis (les tapis)	rug, carpet
le taxi	taxi
la tente	tent
le timbre	stamp
les toilettes (publiques) [f]	(public) washrooms
tourner	to turn
tout droit	straight ahead
le train	train
le trajet	trip
le trajet jusqu'à ... dure ...	the trip to ... takes ...
le tramway	streetcar
le traveller's chèque	traveler's check
treize	thirteen
trente	thirty
trois	three
troisième	third
tu	you
tu viens d'où?	where do you come from?
un/une	a, one
la vache	cow
le vélo	bicycle
venir	to come
le verre	glass
vert(e)	green
la ville	town
vingt	twenty
vingt-deux	twenty-two
vingt et un	twenty-one
la visite	tour, visit
visiter	to visit (a place)
la voiture	car
votre	your
vous	you
vous avez?	do you have?
vous venez d'où?	where do you come from?

1993 Printing
First published in 1993 by Passport Books, a Division of NTC Publishing Group, 4255 W. Touhy Avenue, Lincolnwood, IL 60646–1975 USA.
© 1993 NTC Publishing Group and Usborne Publishing, Ltd.